I Can Write

Letters and Emails

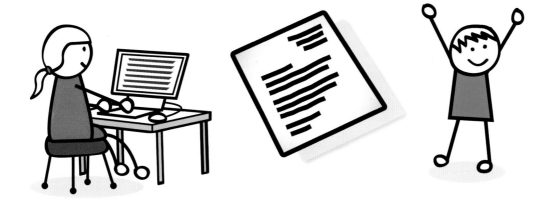

Anita Ganeri

www.raintreepublishers.co.uk
Visit our website to find out more information about Raintree books.

To order:
☎ Phone 0845 6044371
🖨 Fax +44 (0) 1865 312263
💻 Email myorders@raintreepublishers.co.uk

Customers from outside the UK please telephone +44 1865 312262

Raintree is an imprint of Capstone Global Library Limited, a company incorporated in England and Wales having its registered office at 7 Pilgrim Street, London, EC4V 6LB – Registered company number: 6695582

Text © Capstone Global Library Limited 2013
First published in hardback in 2013
The moral rights of the proprietor have been asserted.

Edited by Daniel Nunn, Rebecca Rissman, and Sian Smith
Designed by Victoria Allen
Picture research by Elizabeth Alexander
Original illustrations © Capstone Global Library Ltd 2013
Illustrated by Victoria Allen and Darren Lingard
Production by Victoria Fitzgerald
Originated by Capstone Global Library Ltd
Printed and bound in China by Leo Paper Products Ltd

ISBN 978 1 406 23832 7
16 15 14 13 12
10 9 8 7 6 5 4 3 2 1

British Library Cataloguing in Publication Data
Ganeri, Anita, 1961-
 Letters and emails. -- (I can write)
 1. Letters--Juvenile literature. 2. Letter writing--Juvenile literature. 3. Electronic mail messages--Juvenile literature.
 I. Title II. Series
 808.6-dc23

Acknowledgements
We would like to thank the following for permission to reproduce photographs and artworks: Alamy pp.7 (© Jack Sullivan), 24 (© imagebroker), 25 (© Caro); Corbis p.5 (© Renee Lynn); Shutterstock pp.4 (© Darrin Henry), 6 (© KariDesign), 7 (© Goodluz), 8 (© notkoo), 9 (© EDHAR), 10 (© Feng Yu), 10 (© Vishnevskiy Vasily), 10 (© Chas), 11 (© Elena Schweitzer), 12 (© PeJo), 15 (© Ramona Heim), 17 (© Lorelyn Medina), 17 (© gladcov), 18 (© photosync), 19 (© lev dolgachov), 20 (© Selyutina Olga), 21 (© mattasbestos), 23 (© 75621280), 26 (© fusebulb), 27 (© iadams), 27 (© PePl).

Every effort has been made to contact copyright holders of material reproduced in this book. Any omissions will be rectified in subsequent printings if notice is given to the publisher.

Disclaimer
All the internet addresses (URLs) given in this book were valid at the time of going to press. However, due to the dynamic nature of the internet, some addresses may have changed, or sites may have changed or ceased to exist since publication. While the author and publisher regret any inconvenience this may cause readers, no responsibility for any such changes can be accepted by either the author or the publisher.

Contents

Some words are shown in bold, **like this**. You can find out what they mean in the glossary on page 30.

What is writing?

When you put words on paper or on a computer screen, you are writing. It is important to be able to write clearly so that readers can understand what you mean.

What do you like writing about?

Letters are delivered to your door.

There are many different types of writing. This book is about letters. Letters are a type of **non-fiction**. This means that they are about facts and real life.

What are letters?

A letter sends its reader a message or tells them some information. The writer puts the letter in an envelope and sends it by post.

We put stamps on letters so that we can send them by post.

People on holiday send postcards.

Sending an email is quick and easy.

Other ways of sending a message are to write a postcard or **email**. An email is a type of letter that you write on a computer. Then you send it to the reader's computer.

Different letters

There are lots of different types of letters. People write letters to say thank you, invite someone to a party, tell someone some important news, or just catch up with friends.

Party invites are fun to write.

You are invited to my party on 20th August at 5.00 p.m. Please come to 7 Park Road, Tea Town.

A job application needs to be neat and clear.

People also write letters to apply for jobs or to complain when something goes wrong. Sometimes, it is quicker to write an **email** instead.

Writing style

When you are writing a letter, think about the person you are writing to. If you are writing to someone you do not know, use a **formal** style of writing.

Use polite language, such as 'I would', when you are writing a formal letter.

Dear Mr Fisher,
I would like to
become a member of
your birdwatching club…

If you are writing to someone you know, use a more **informal**, chatty style of writing. Always make sure that your writing is clear and easy to understand.

Use chatty language, such as 'Thanks', when you are writing an informal letter.

Dear Aunty Jan,
Thanks for my brilliant
present. I love it!

Laying out a letter

It is important to set your letter out in the right way. This makes it easier to understand. On the opposite page, you can see how to **lay out** a **formal** letter. How to write an **address** on an envelope is shown below.

Mrs Jones
The Supermarket
Brook Street
Seatown
BH7 0PL

7 Oak Tree Road
Seatown
BH4 9NK

12 May 2012

The Supermarket
Brook Street
Seatown
BH7 0PL

Dear Mrs Jones,

I am writing to complain about the bananas I bought from your shop last week. They were very soft and brown. They tasted horrible.

I look forward to hearing from you.

Yours sincerely,
Jack Walton

Starting and ending

There are different ways of starting and ending letters. Here, you can see how to start and end a **formal** letter to someone you do not know.

Dear (person's name),

Yours sincerely,

If you know the person's name, end with 'Yours sincerely'.

Dear Sir or Madam,

Yours faithfully,

If you do not know the person's name, end with 'Yours faithfully'.

Here, you can see how to start and end an **informal** letter to someone you know well.

Dear (person's name),

Best wishes/Love from/
Lots of love,

Use 'Love from' or 'Lots of love' if you know the person really well.

Letter to a penfriend

Imagine that you are writing a letter to a **penfriend**. You are writing to make friends. You may have never met your penfriend but you can still make your letter quite chatty.

Make your letter quite **informal** and friendly. You do not need to write the other person's **address** in an informal letter.

Flat 32, Blue Towers, Longbridge, LN10 3NX

5 September 2012

Dear Gabriela,

How are you? I am your new penfriend. My name is Lucy.

Think about what you want to say in your letter. Your penfriend may live in another country. Their life may be very different to yours.

Here are some things you might want to tell your penfriend. Ask them some questions, too.

Things to write about

- **yourself**
- **your family**
- **your pets**
- **your school**
- **your hobbies**

Thank-you letter

Try writing a letter to thank your aunt for your birthday present. Start off your letter by saying why you are writing and why you like the present.

A thank-you letter can be chatty and **informal**.

Dear Aunty Liz,
Thank you very much
for the lovely crayons
you sent me for my
birthday. They were
just what I wanted…

Sometimes, you might have to say thank you for a present you did not like! How can you be polite about it? Here are some words to help you describe the present.

Can you think of any more useful words?

Useful words

interesting

unusual

surprising

kind

fascinating

Formal letter

You are writing a **formal** letter to your local zoo. You want them to help you with a school project. Plan what you are going to say before you start writing.

Useful tips

- **Explain why you are writing.**
- **Explain how they can help you.**
- **Thank them for reading your letter.**
- **Use the correct beginning and ending.**

You might want to enclose a **SAE** (stamped addressed envelope) with your letter. Write your own **address** on the envelope and stick on a stamp.

A SAE is useful if you want someone to reply. It saves them the trouble of finding an envelope or buying a stamp.

Holly Alston
Ashfields Primary School
Ashfields
AS9 76T

Sending a postcard

People often write postcards when they go on holiday. You write your short message on the left-hand side. You write the reader's **address** on the right-hand side.

Make sure that you leave room for the address.

Hi there!

Having a great time. Hotel is wicked, with huge pool. Going surfing tomorrow. Wish you were here. See you soon!

Love Asif

Charlie Parker
1 Manley Road
Wurnley
WX1 1XW

You can write a postcard in an **informal** way. There is not much space on a postcard, so you can leave out your address and a greeting.

Things you might say

- **where you are**
- **what you have been doing**
- **what the weather is like**

Here are a few things you could say.

How email works

An **email** is a letter or note that you send on a computer. 'Email' is short for 'electronic mail'. An email is very quick and easy to send.

Writing an email is a quick way of sending a message.

To send an email to someone, type in their **email address**. Then write your message and press 'Send'. Press 'Reply' to answer an email that someone has sent to you.

Always read your email again before you send it. Once you click 'Send', it is too late to change it!

Writing an email

Like letters, **emails** can be **formal** or **informal**. Begin a formal email with 'Dear…' and end it with 'Yours sincerely' or 'Yours faithfully'.

> The date appears **automatically** in the email.

To: D.Robinson@Museum.com
Subject: School trip
Date: Wed, 24 Oct 2012

Dear Miss Robinson,

We really enjoyed our visit to your museum last week. Thank you for looking after us.

Yours sincerely,

Izzy Price

Emails to friends are informal and chatty. You can write them in note form. You can start them with 'Hi' and end them with 'Love from' or 'See you soon'.

An informal email is like a note.

To: Joe6@no.address.com
Subject: Party
Date: Fri, 16 Nov 2012

Hi Joe!

Party tomorrow afternoon – can you come?

See you soon,

Luke

27

Top tips for writing letters and emails

1. If you are writing a **formal** letter, make sure that your handwriting is neat and easy to read. You can also write it on a computer.

2. Read through your letter or **email** before you send it. Check your spelling and correct anything that is wrong.

3. Keep your **sentences** short in a letter, especially if it is to someone you do not know. This makes it easy to read and understand.

4. Before you write your letter, make a quick note of what you want to say.

This is especially useful if you are writing a letter to complain about something.

5. Write your letter on ruled, or lined, paper. This will help to keep your writing in straight lines and make your letter look neater.

6. When you are replying to a letter, write a rough copy first. Make sure that you answer any points or questions in the letter.

7. If you see the letters 'RSVP' on an invitation, it means 'please reply'. This will help the sender to plan their party.

8. Keep practising! Writing is like playing tennis or football. You need to keep practising.

Glossary

address where a person lives, including house number, street name, and city or town

automatically without you having to do anything

email letter that you write and send on a computer. 'Email' is short for 'electronic mail'.

email address the address you use when you want to send someone an email

formal language that is correct and follows the rules

informal language that is more friendly and breaks some of the rules

lay out to set out a letter on a piece of paper in a clear way

non-fiction writing that is about real people or things

penfriend friend you write to, even though you may never have met them

SAE stamped addressed envelope. A stamped addressed envelope is an envelope with your own address on and a stamp.

sentence group of words that makes sense on its own

Find out more

Books

Getting to Grips with Grammar, Anita Ganeri
(Raintree Publishing, 2012)

How to Write Letters and Emails, Celia Warren
(QED Publishing, 2008)

Websites

www.bbc.co.uk/schools/ks1bitesize/literacy

www.bbc.co.uk/schools/ks2bitesize/english/writing

Index